Origins

Message in an X-bot

Tony Bradman • Jonatronix

OXFORD
UNIVERSITY PRESS

Previously ...

In the book *The Thing in the Cupboard*, micro-sized Tiger meets a strange robot. It looks like a scary metal spider.

Tiger escapes but the Thing gets squashed.
Max asks Miss Jones if he can try and fix it.

Miss Jones thinks the Thing is just a toy.
Max is not so sure …

Chapter 1 – A strange little robot

After school, Max took the Thing home and started to work on it. He soon got the legs straight and put the body back into shape. But the Thing didn't move or make a sound.

He looked at it closely. Was it some sort of tiny robot? Tiger said it had chased him. It was a mystery.

What was it? Where had it come from?

Max knew that Ant would know what to do.
So he called Ant and asked him to come round.

"Wow, that is so cool!" said Ant when he saw
the little robot. He grabbed it off Max and looked
at it closely. "What does X1 NASTI mean?"
he asked, pointing to the front of the robot.

Max shrugged.

"OK," said Ant. "If I can fix it, can I keep it?"

"No, you can't," said Max, grabbing the Thing back. He wanted to keep the robot.

"Fine," Ant snapped. "Fix it yourself, then."

That evening Max spent ages working on the robot. Still the robot didn't move or make a sound. Max knew it was no good being cross with Ant. He needed his help.

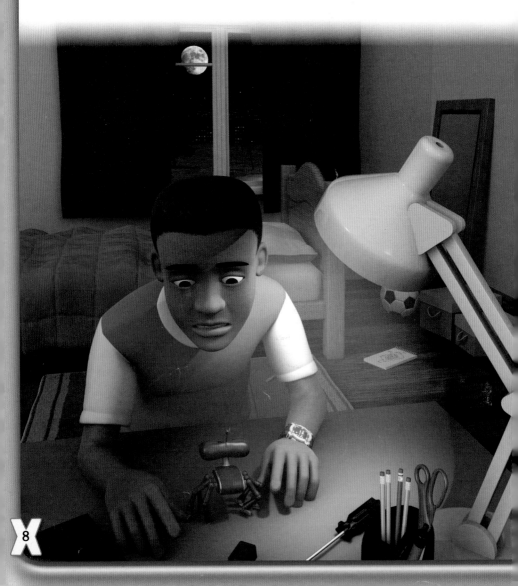

The next morning, Max called Ant. There was no answer. So he sent a text message.

Ant, pls help! Robot still not moving. Can't fix it without u. :-(

Ant did not reply. Then Max had an idea.

Max took lots of pictures of the robot. Then he uploaded them to his computer and emailed them to Ant.

Let's get it fixed first, Max wrote in the message. *We can talk later about who keeps it. Come on, Ant, please …*

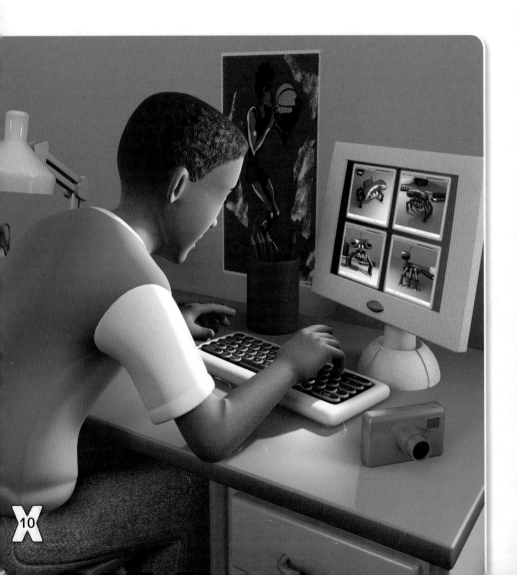

Ant stared at the pictures of the robot. What was it? There was only one way to find out. He was cross with Max but he *knew* that they could fix it if they worked together.

OK, he replied. *Meet me at the micro-den in half an hour.*

Chapter 3 – Working together

When Max got to the micro-den, Ant was there waiting for him.

"What's your plan, then?" said Max.

"It's very simple," said Ant. "I think something small inside the robot is broken. It will be easier for us to fix if we are small, too."

"Now why didn't I think of that?" said Max, impressed.

The boys turned the dials on their watches and …

Max and Ant pulled the robot into their den. Ant looked inside the robot. He soon found out what was wrong.

Ant told Max what tools he needed and Max handed them to his friend.

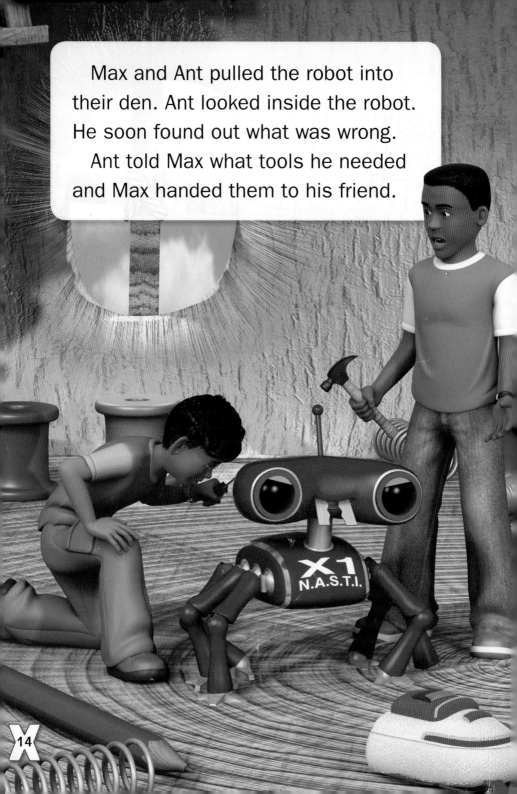

"That's done it," said Ant at last.

He pressed a switch. There was a humming noise and the robot's eyes lit up. Then it lurched forwards …

Chapter 4 – Trapped!

Max and Ant backed away, but the robot kept coming. It hummed and buzzed and clicked and clacked its jaws.

"Oh, no!" cried Max. "Tiger said it chased him in the cupboard."

"Why didn't you tell me that before?"
groaned Ant. "Let's try and get past ..."

The boys made for the door – but the robot
scuttled across and cut them off. It forced
them back against the wall.

Suddenly the robot stopped.

"I have a message for you," it said in a strange voice. A beam of light shot out of it … and before them stood the image of a young woman.

"Wow, it's a hologram!" said Ant.

"I haven't got long to make this recording," said the young woman. "And I hope the X1 gets it to you. All I can say is – beware of Dr X!"

Then the image fizzed like a TV going wrong … and vanished.

Chapter 5 – Play it again, Ant

"What was all that about?" said Ant. "Who is she? And who is Dr X?"

"I don't know," said Max. "But it must be important. Can you get the message to play again? We need to show it to Tiger and Cat."

"No problem," said Ant with a smile. "Can I keep the robot now? I think I'll call it Rover."

Max smiled back at his friend. Ant deserved to keep the robot.

What Max, Cat, Ant and Tiger didn't know is that they would soon be seeing many more of these strange little robots …

Find out more ...

To find out more about communication, read *The Deadly Boomslang*

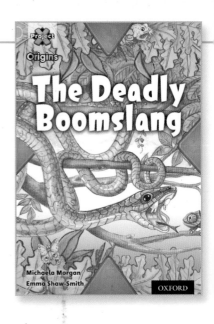

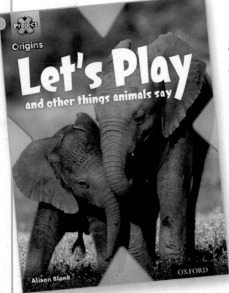

and *Let's Play and other things animals say*.